ILLUMIN^TIONS

WISDOM FROM
THIS PLANET'S
GREATEST MINDS

1

ILLUMINATIONS

WISDOM FROM
THIS PLANET'S
GREATEST MINDS

Design: LIRIM
Photography: Shutterstock

ISBN: 978-0-9972758-0-3

First Edition: February 2016
10 9 8 7 6 5 4 3 2 1

CONTENTS

WISDOM IS A KEY TO WEALTH, HEALTH, AND HAPPINESS

More valuable than knowledge, wisdom is gained by learning from the past to find solutions in the present.

ILLUMINATIONS IS A COMPASS FOR ALL WHO SEEK LIVES OF GREATNESS

By examining the words of presidents, philosophers, billionaires, and thought leaders, any person can bridge the gap between where they are and where they are meant to be.

READ THE ILLUMINATIONS IN ORDER OR CHOOSE ANY PAGE

Start at the beginning, or browse the contents when seeking guidance on specific topics.

REFLECT ON THE ILLUMINATIONS OFTEN

They have been chosen carefully and contain many meanings. Spend time thinking about each Illumination and ways you can apply its insights to your life.

POWER &
LEADERSHIP

A crown,

golden in show,
is but a
wreath
of

thorns.

JOHN MILTON

Do you desire to be a leader, or are you merely a seeker of the power and privileges that leaders receive? The people may see their king on a throne and wonder why one human is allowed to reign above another — believing that they are deserving of a life they believe to be easy.

But when war comes to their gates, will they have the courage to decide whose children must be sent to fight and die, and whose will stay and live? When the crown of a prince's father and grandfather adorns his head, will he be able to defend their citizens? When you answer to no one, no one answers your cries for help.

It is easy to strive for the benefits of power while overlooking their great responsibilities. If you are meant to be a leader, seek wisdom over riches. Those with power and no wisdom often lose it; those with wisdom and no power often gain it.

A LEADER
IS ONE WHO
KNOWS THE WAY,
GOES THE WAY, AND
SHOWS THE WAY.

JOHN MAXWELL

Leaders enjoy the privileges of wealth and power and prestige, but also must bear the burden of responsibilities that followers can never understand. The leader has no one to follow — no one to say which way to go and which path to avoid. They must forge ahead with certainty, calculating every possible outcome to ensure the safety of those who walk behind them.

The lives of millions rest in a leader's hands. Are you prepared to lead when times are hard and others look to you for direction? Are you certain that you will point them the right way?

A MAN WHO WANTS TO LEAD THE ORCHESTRA MUST TURN HIS BACK ON THE CROWD

MAX LUCADO

A leader cannot lead and follow at the same time. Followers seek riches and glory for their own satisfaction, focusing on their own desires rather than the needs of the people around them. Leaders look beyond the trappings of personal gain, knowing that their decisions affect the lives of all who look to them for guidance and direction.

True leaders give little attention to the shallow material pleasures that surround their palaces and offices: gold and silks are merely decorum to prove the prosperity of the people they represent. Followers seek glory and riches without the responsibility they carry. If you wish to lead, first you must cease to follow.

IF YOU WANT
TO SEE THE
TRUE MEASURE
OF A MAN,
WATCH HOW
HE TREATS
HIS INFERIORS,
NOT HIS EQUALS.

J. K. ROWLING

The soul of every human is equal but their bodies are never the same. Some are born rich while others are born poor; some are strong while others are weak. Equality is a mythical goal — striving for it is honorable but attaining it is impossible. Some will always be superior to others. Even the weak are stronger than the dead.

However, it is the duty of every human to treat each other as if all are at the same level, for every person has the opportunity to become greater. Those who are weak now can become stronger in time. Every person — regardless of their current stature or prestige — should be treated in a manner befitting their potential. The podium of judgment that looks down upon the weak is a pedestal that is easily toppled.

lions
DON'T LOSE
SLEEP OVER THE
opinions
OF SHEEP

The life of a sheep is easier than the life of a lion. Sheep are given food and water freely by their shepherd, protected from predators and threats by shelters they did not build.

But these comforts bind the sheep into slavery. The sheep are bred to be weaker of mind and body, to require the shepherd's protection so greatly that they can be free of chains but never stray. Theirs is a lifetime of servitude — one that is comfortable but ends at the shepherd's whim.

Lions have no masters. Though the lion must hunt for its own food and search for its own shelter, it is free to roam where it desires and requires permission from no one. It follows any path it chooses. The sheep may yell in an echoing multitude but the lion's roar will silence them in an instant.

Some humans are sheep. They rely on others for their comforts, doing as little as possible and striving for nothing. They scream in protest when they are fenced in and herded — angry that they are not free like the lions — but accept the shepherd's food nonetheless.

Leaders must have unwavering confidence. They pay no heed to the voices of human sheep who taunt them — bragging of their lives of ease, criticizing any who strive to be better, yelling that all deserve equal rewards for unequal effort.

Is it the lion's stupidity that keeps it from a life of leisure? How can so many sheep be wrong as they grow fatter on the shepherd's food? Why would any creature choose to run free in the dangerous and uncertain wilderness?

At sunset, the sheep are herded back into their prison and fed in abundance until they drift into sleep. The lion enjoys no such promises of food or shelter, wandering upon the mountains in search of a meal to ease its hunger.

Humans are not born as sheep or lions and must choose a path for themselves. Will they strive for what is easy and safe, to follow close to the multitude, to remain within the fences that protect them from the outside but imprison them within its boundaries? Or will they travel the path they choose for themselves, running freely in the dangerous wildernesses of life, leading their own way in a planet filled with followers?

Though it lacks the comforts of a shepherd's security, a lion never wishes for the life of a sheep. A lion may hunger while a sheep is fed but the fattest sheep is the lion's meal.

FAME &
PRESTIGE

AFTER I'M DEAD
I'D RATHER HAVE
PEOPLE ASK

WHY I HAVE NO MONUMENT

THAN WHY
I HAVE ONE

CATO THE ELDER

Many kings have ordered for statues to be built in honor of their victories, only to have them torn down after their lives have ended. Who benefits from the endless heralding of one's own successes? If one is truly great, others will proclaim their greatness for them.

Though you may see wealth and happiness in your life, focus on what you can continue to do rather than what you have done. It is wise to be proud of your achievements, but allow your reputation to speak of your magnificence instead of your words.

Seekers of glory vanish the quickest. Build a better life for those around you and they will build your monument.

FAME

USUALLY COMES TO THOSE WHO ARE

THINKING ABOUT SOMETHING ELSE.

OLIVER WENDELL HOLMES

The successful do not dwell on the opinions of reporters and fanatics. To the famous, fame is merely a side effect of their greatest achievements. Flashing lights and cameras are tools of the trade: windows for the public to gaze through as they search for people and things to seize their attention. Fame is simply a pedestal lifting up objects for others to desire.

Seekers of fame rarely find good fortune. Instead, choose to create something that will be desired by many, and they will lift you up into the heights of prominence on their own shoulders.

*IT IS DANGEROUS
TO LET THE PUBLIC
BEHIND THE
SCENES.
THEY ARE EASILY
DISILLUSIONED
AND THEN THEY
ARE ANGRY WITH
YOU, FOR IT WAS
THE ILLUSION
THEY LOVED.*

W. SOMERSET MAUGHAM

Many wish to look through the windows of the wealthy and powerful to study the recipe to their success. But those who have seen the inner workings of power are often disillusioned by their normalcy — imagining that there must be secrets and mysteries but finding tedious simplicity instead.

Though a queen speaks in front of millions, hundreds of assistants hide behind the curtains to ensure that she sounds and appears flawless. Every detail is planned and perfected to maintain the illusion that a star is better than others around them. Though the people desire to see behind the curtain, their disappointment is inevitable: a person's imagination is often more thrilling than reality.

GLORY IS LIKE A CIRCLE IN THE WATER WHICH NEVER CEASES TO ENLARGE ITSELF, TILL, BY BROAD SPREADING, IT DISPERSES TO NAUGHT.

WILLIAM SHAKESPEARE

Beware the seductive voice of glory. A single taste begins its addiction, driving a desire for more and more each day. Its first touch is like a finger pressing into a still pool of water, creating a ripple that grows larger until it reaches the edges. Once the ripple disappears, the stillness of the water suddenly seems insufficient to eyes that have already seen its movement. Like fame and glory, it yearns for more, the finger pressing into it again and again until the water bounces with waves reverberating in all directions. Soon the water is merely a violent tempest — as are the lives of the seekers of glory.

If you seek power, prepare for its seductions. Though many fools drown in glory's pool, the cautious emerge clean.

FAME *IS AN ILLUSIVE THING – HERE TODAY, GONE TOMORROW.*

THE FICKLE, SHALLOW MOB RAISES ITS HEROES TO THE PINNACLE OF APPROVAL TODAY AND HURLS THEM INTO OBLIVION TOMORROW AT THE SLIGHTEST WHIM;

CHEERS TODAY, HISSES TOMORROW; UTTER FORGETFULNESS IN A FEW MONTHS.

HENRY MILLER

Seekers of fame often find it but lose it just as quickly. Glory is built upon the whims of others — a never-ending facade that claims one person is better than another. It requires the attention of many to be focused on the actions of one.

But there are many others who seek such attention, and their voices and achievements can suddenly grow like a tree that leaves your deeds lost in its shadow. When the eyes of the crowd have turned away, will you be left with anything?

Fame and prestige are fickle companions. Enjoy their company but never their loyalty. Seek them only if you are prepared for their eventual abandonment, and build more with your life than a monument that vanishes in the shadow of another's.

LOVE &
RELATIONSHIPS

OUR CHIEF
WANT IN LIFE IS

SOMEBODY

WHO WILL
MAKE US

DO WHAT
WE CAN

RALPH WALDO EMERSON

Every person is born with hopes and goals but only a few fully attain them. Though they begin with great expectations, many people are distracted from their intended path by hardships, time, and money — some for so long that they never return to the road that leads to their dreams. Though they may have the ability to reach the end, they lose the determination to continue their journey.

Your choice in companions can mean the difference between a life veering further from the path and a partnership that steers each other back to the center. The love of another person can strengthen, guide, and empower even those who have been lost in the mires of self-doubt. When chosen wisely, love can navigate even the most complicated of life's maps.

LOVE

IS FRIENDSHIP THAT HAS

CAUGHT FIRE.

IT IS QUIET **UNDERSTANDING**,
MUTUAL **CONFIDENCE**,
SHARING AND **FORGIVING**.

IT IS **LOYALTY** THROUGH
GOOD AND BAD TIMES.

IT SETTLES FOR
LESS THAN PERFECTION
AND MAKES ALLOWANCES FOR
HUMAN WEAKNESSES.

ANN LANDERS

Love at first sight is rarely more than lust: a powerful attractant but a weak foundation. Desire is fleeting and unpredictable, like a torch in the wind. Can its flame survive the battering of failures, disagreements, mistrust, and hardship? Will it continue burning through the harshest times or will it vanish, leaving its carriers lost in the darkness?

Friendship is the strongest bond of love. When meshed with attraction, it pulls together lives like the pieces of a home. Beauty and riches are only polished exteriors that captivate when all is calm, but go forgotten when lightning strikes. As winds batter the house and time takes its toll, the outside begins to fade. The color loses its shine. The beauty loses its glow. But even in the most violent of tempests, a strong foundation can weather life's many storms, and protect those who find shelter in its unity.

DO NOT THINK THAT

LOVE

IN ORDER TO
BE GENUINE
HAS TO BE
EXTRAORDINARY.

WHAT WE NEED IS
TO LOVE WITHOUT
GETTING TIRED.

BE FAITHFUL
IN SMALL THINGS

BECAUSE IT IS
IN THEM THAT
YOUR STRENGTH LIES.

MOTHER TERESA

It is tempting to believe that love is made of lavish deeds. The happiest relationships may appear to thrive on outward perfection but only because the grandest moments of a relationship are shown to outsiders, while the quieter moments are kept within.

A flower that is watered only once a week will surely wither and die of thirst. A person who feasts once per month, but eats nothing every other day, will surely starve.

Love requires constant cultivation to remain alive. Extravagant gestures may plant it but small, constant affirmations give it strength. With daily time and attention, true love can bloom from a tiny seed.

*AN ACT
OF LOVE THAT
FAILS IS JUST AS
MUCH A PART OF
THE DIVINE LIFE AS
AN ACT OF LOVE
THAT SUCCEEDS,
FOR LOVE IS
MEASURED BY
FULLNESS
NOT BY RECEPTION.*

HAROLD LOUKES

Broken hearts cause more pain than open wounds. Love unreturned is like a venom that lingers in a person's mind and soul, sapping their strength away with endless questions: Why not me? What am I doing wrong? Will I ever be enough?

Love is a gift. When a gift is unwanted, is the giver to blame?

Find strength in refusals. Love that is denied always returns to its sender, ready to be given to another who deserves it. Cultivate love not as a single tree but as a garden to be shared with those who accept it. A heart is broken by love, but the same love rebuilds it anew.

love

WILL FIND A WAY

INDIFFERENCE

WILL FIND AN EXCUSE.

When you love someone, it can be difficult to realize when they do not love you back. Disloyalty, harshness, and apathy can be brushed aside and ignored when seen through eyes clouded with affection. Far too many hearts are blind-sided by betrayal, missing the clues because they did not want to see them.

Recognize love by actions, not promises. Love is counterfeit when marked with repeated apologies for unfaithfulness and shallow gifts meant to distract from wrong-doing. Love should be obvious even in the face of hardships and disagreements — a free-flowing river that is given without stipulation or threat.

If love is real, there should be no uncertainty of its existence. A person who truly loves you will make sure it is known every day of your life.

WEALTH &
SUCCESS

A GREAT FORTUNE IN THE HANDS OF A FOOL IS A GREAT MISFORTUNE.

ANONYMOUS

Wealth befalls the foolish and the wise, but only the wise are able to keep it. A person who lacks an understanding of money's consequences is like a child prince who inherits a kingdom: a slave to whims, easily manipulated, and quick to fall from power. To attain riches but lose it all is far more painful than never having riches at all.

If you currently lack wealth, consider it a temporary blessing. Use this time as your prequel. Pursue knowledge and wisdom so that when money enters your life, you are prepared to face its responsibilities.

Failures are lessons that are hard to forget. When you have little to lose, a misstep is merely an error; when you have much on the line, a mistake can cause your downfall.

NOTHING IS ENOUGH FOR THE MAN TO WHOM ENOUGH IS TOO LITTLE.

EPICURUS

How many palaces must a person own to be happy? From afar, wealth may appear to be the answer to all of life's problems. In sickness, wealth can buy doctors. In fear, wealth can buy protection. Even in sadness, wealth can buy temporary comforts.

But wealth cannot buy happiness. Money is quicksand — a slow entrapment for those who do not escape soon enough. It is expensive to be rich. Your mansion must maintain staff. Your private jet must be housed in a hangar. As an obsession with wealth overtakes a person's life, soon money becomes the master and its owner becomes the servant.

Like an addiction, a little wealth always wants more. Seek worthy investments that promise greater returns over time. Appreciate what you have and you will never lose what you are given.

on the soft bed
of luxury many
kingdoms have
expired

ANDREW YOUNG

The taste of wealth is a sweet poison. It pulls a person deep into its vortex, enticing them with promises of comfort and ease. What purpose does work serve when a person has enough to never work again? Why strive for anything when you have everything?

But as time goes on, "everything" begins to feel like nothing. A life lacking purpose is a life lacking direction. Palaces and planes cannot fill the void of an aimlessly wandering soul.

When wealth enters your life, resist the temptations of luxury. Use money as a tool to achieve greater things and to bring positive changes to the lives around you. Wealth is never the finish line but merely another step in life's journey.

WEALTH
IS AN INBORN ATTITUDE OF
MIND

THE PAUPER WHO
HAS MADE HIS PILE
MAY FLAUNT HIS
SPOILS, BUT CANNOT
WEAR THEM PLAUSIBLY.

JEAN COCTEAU

Wealth in the hands of the unwise is like a golden crown on a pig. Flashy cars and sprawling estates can be purchased by anyone who can afford them, but respect is not for sale. When a person lacks wisdom, money is merely a magnifying glass that focuses all attention to their weaknesses. No amount of riches can disguise a fool.

Become familiar with the good and bad aspects of wealth. Study those who have succeeded and fallen before you. Though money may unlock doors, it cannot guarantee a welcome inside. The truly rich have no need to flaunt their wealth: their inner confidence speaks louder than gold and diamonds. As you seek riches, pursue the wisdom required to keep it.

GREAT MINDS DISCUSS IDEAS; AVERAGE MINDS DISCUSS EVENTS; SMALL MINDS DISCUSS PEOPLE

ELEANOR ROOSEVELT

Many words are wasted in time that could be spent in action. Endless discussion of wealth and power brings you no closer to either. Speaking badly of those who have attained the things you seek only separates you further from them. Money does not come to those who call its name the most. Gossip's only beneficiary is the one being gossiped about.

Instead, use jealousy as an endless well of motivation. Do you see the wealthy and wish for their lives of luxury and affluence? Do you see the elite and wish for their voices that call the attention of millions? Use their headlines and successes as inspirational fuel that drives you toward the goals you seek.

KNOWLEDGE
& WISDOM

A LOVE AFFAIR WITH KNOWLEDGE WILL NEVER END IN HEARTBREAK

MICHAEL GARRETT MARINO

Every action a person takes is reliant upon their judgment — the understanding, knowledge, and wisdom that make up their internal compass. Your ability to make choices can mean the difference between polarizing outcomes: wealth or poverty, sickness or health, conflict or peace. Every aspect of your life depends on the soundness of your mind.

The human brain works like an internal supercomputer, processing all available information when faced with decisions. Knowledge is software for the brain. Every piece of information adds new abilities and perspectives to a person's inner guide, ready to be called upon when they are needed.

An investment in knowledge is the safest of life's gambles. Money may vanish but knowledge lives forever.

A WISE MAN KNOWS HOW LITTLE HE KNOWS

ANONYMOUS

In life, there is no end to the lessons that can be learned. Wisdom is not a task that can be completed or a race that can be won. It is a constant development that lasts a lifetime. Every day is a chance to gain experience. Every mistake is an opportunity to learn something new.

To cease the pursuit of wisdom is to walk in a straight line through a dark forest. Arrogance refuses the help of maps or the guidance of others, forging onward and looking only in the direction ahead. Though signs point in warning, a foolish person is too blinded by pride to observe their surroundings — too oblivious to see the cliff's edge in front of them until it is too late.

The wisest study their successes to find what they should repeat, and study their failures to avoid the same mistakes. Heed the warnings and lessons throughout life, and they will guide you to safety.

BE CURIOUS ALWAYS!
FOR KNOWLEDGE WILL
NOT ACQUIRE YOU:
YOU MUST
ACQUIRE IT

BERTRAND RUSSELL

Every great discovery is the child of determination and curiosity. A yearning to understand the mysteries of this universe drives a person along the never-ending pathway of knowledge.

Curiosity begins with questions. How does that work? What does that mean? Why does that happen?

Look past the surface of everything. Encourage yourself to wonder and to question. You are surrounded by puzzles waiting to be solved — each answer reveals knowledge that can be used for the rest of your life.

IT IS ALWAYS SAFE TO LEARN, EVEN FROM OUR ENEMIES; SELDOM SAFE TO VENTURE TO INSTRUCT, EVEN OUR FRIENDS.

CHARLES CALEB COLTON

A leader's greatest strength is knowing his greatest weakness. No person is made perfect and every human is born with unique flaws that affect every decision they make. For some it is envy. For others, greed. And for many, it is pride.

Enemies are often more honest than friends. Friends will overlook your weaknesses, telling you what you want to hear instead of what you should be told because they see you through eyes clouded by admiration.

Enemies care nothing for your friendship. A rival will find your most vulnerable point and expose it without any remorse. But this is a gift — a chance to strengthen where you are weak. A fortress that cannot withstand the storm will never survive the hurricane.

KNOWLEDGE
IS ANCIENT ERROR
REFLECTING ON
ITS YOUTH

FRANCIS PICABIA

Much can be learned from the mistakes of the past. A child who reaches for the tempting glow of a fire learns a haunting lesson that will prevent him from burning himself again as an adult. Doctors of the past made mistakes that killed thousands of patients, but the discoveries made from these deaths now spare the lives of thousands every day.

Look back on your mistakes and the lessons you can learn from them. How could you have acted differently? If you were faced with the same decision today, could you change the outcome? Do not be afraid to face the decisions you wish you could undo. If not for error, there would be no progress.

CHOICES & DECISIONS

WHENEVER YOU
FIND YOURSELF
ON THE SIDE OF THE
MAJORITY
IT IS TIME TO PAUSE

—— & ——

REFLECT

MARK TWAIN

The minds of the people are easily swayed by the pressures of hardship. Their decisions become clouded by fears that cause them to take actions out of desperation — actions they know are wrong but become easier to commit when their resolve has been chipped away. Mob mentality is a vacuum that pulls people with good intentions toward a destructive center, convincing them to do harmful things they would never consider alone.

When the voices of hundreds shout that the city must burn, it becomes harder to hear the thousands who quietly disagree. A leader cannot fall prey to the whims of the voices that shout the loudest, but must stand as a voice of reason in defense of the silent.

I HAVE NOT FAILED.

I'VE JUST FOUND

10,000 WAYS

THAT WON'T WORK.

THOMAS EDISON

All great things are done through dedication. The builders of the pyramids began with a single stone and continued until every piece was in place. The skills of the most proficient designers were sharpened by the pain of their worst mistakes.

A person must look a thousand ways before choosing a direction, and walk a hundred steps before deciding which is the right path. Determination and perseverance can survive even 10,000 failures, and hope promises victory in the end.

LIVE AS IF
YOU WERE TO
DIE TOMORROW.
LEARN AS IF
YOU WERE TO
LIVE FOREVER.

MAHATMA GANDHI

When you are faced with difficult decisions, ask yourself which way you would choose if tomorrow was the last day of your life. Is the disagreement with your friend worth the distance it is creating between you? Is the cost of a new house worth the time you must spend working to pay for it? If tomorrow was your ending, would today be your best final chapter?

Sometimes, the answer is yes. The importance is in the question itself.

DON'T LET THE
FEAR OF LOSING
BE GREATER THAN
THE EXCITEMENT
OF WINNING

ROBERT KIYOSAKI

You will fail many times in life. You will seek knowledge, pursue goodness, work with the deepest of dedication, and still things will go wrong. The missteps can become overwhelming and lead you to question: is it all worth it if I could still lose in the end?

Victory is never immediate or easy. It always comes at the last expected moment — appearing when your breaking point is nearly reached. If you push aside your fears and stay focused on your ultimate goal, it will feed you the energy you need to power through any obstacles.

IT IS OUR CHOICES THAT SHOW WHAT WE TRULY ARE, FAR MORE THAN OUR ABILITIES

J.K. ROWLING

There have been thousands of kings and queens on this planet, but most are forgotten. Hidden between the names that appear in history books are scores of unheralded royalty whose lives never merited even a sentence of recognition. Though they sat upon the same thrones and wore the same crowns, they are left forgotten behind the names of leaders who chose to take action and create change.

Many people have the ability to become leaders. But ability is not enough. The choices you make determine the direction of your life. Seek out your strengths, but also seek out ways you can use them.

HARDSHIPS
& BRAVERY

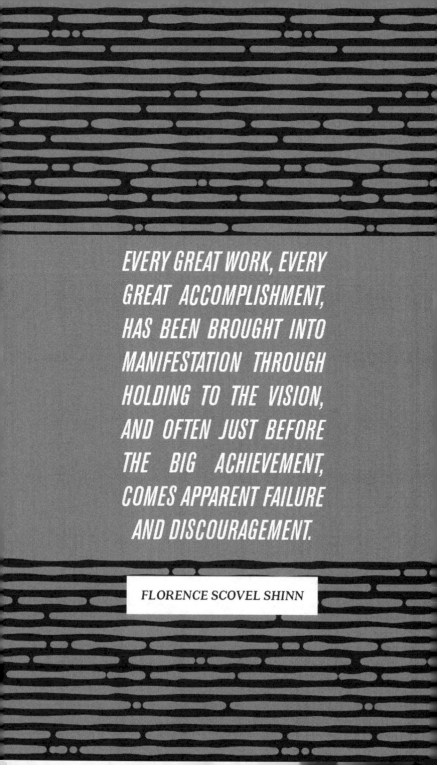

EVERY GREAT WORK, EVERY GREAT ACCOMPLISHMENT, HAS BEEN BROUGHT INTO MANIFESTATION THROUGH HOLDING TO THE VISION, AND OFTEN JUST BEFORE THE BIG ACHIEVEMENT, COMES APPARENT FAILURE AND DISCOURAGEMENT.

FLORENCE SCOVEL SHINN

All successes are found after great difficulty. Hardships are rocks on the road to victory, threatening to tear apart your shoes and tripping you along the way. A person becomes weary as they work on a project, and wearier with each passing moment they spend searching for its solution. Time has a way of cultivating discouragement, steadily chipping away at a person's stamina with self-doubts and internal anxieties.

If winning was easy, winning would be no victory. Magnificent accomplishments require effort and perseverance. When you trip, you must stand again. The harder the journey is, the greater the reward at its end.

THE WOODS
ARE LOVELY,
DARK AND DEEP.
BUT I HAVE
PROMISES
TO KEEP,
AND MILES TO GO
BEFORE I SLEEP.

ROBERT FROST

When facing hardships, it is tempting to stop and dwell on how bad things are. You may work hard and still face financial difficulty. You may love deeply and still be refused. At times it may feel as if all the effort you have dedicated to improving your life has gone to waste when the rewards do not appear as quickly as you expected.

Do not linger to look at the devastation around you or give sadness a chance to weigh you down. Keep walking toward the glow that signals the end of the dark forest. Keep moving ahead until you are free.

WHAT YOU GET
BY ACHIEVING
YOUR GOALS

IS NOT AS
IMPORTANT AS

WHAT YOU **BECOME**
BY ACHIEVING
YOUR GOALS.

ZIG ZIGLAR

A soldier begins without skills or competence, stumbling through training alongside rows of others with similar short-comings. Through years of work and toil, a private steadily climbs the ranks — making less mistakes, sharpening more abilities. With enough dedication, even the lowest of soldiers can become the highest of commanders.

Badges and medals do not make a general. Awards are only reminders of the lessons learned, the skills obtained, the hardships overcome, and the victories finally reached after a lifetime of perseverance. The goal is not found in what waits at the end, but rather in the achievements made along the way.

HERE'S TO THE CRAZY ONES. THE MISFITS. THE REBELS. THE TROUBLEMAKERS. THE ROUND PEGS IN THE SQUARE HOLES. THE ONES WHO SEE THINGS DIFFERENTLY. THEY'RE NOT FOND OF RULES. AND THEY HAVE NO RESPECT FOR THE STATUS QUO. YOU CAN QUOTE THEM, DISAGREE WITH THEM, GLORIFY OR VILIFY THEM. ABOUT THE ONLY THING YOU CAN'T DO IS IGNORE THEM. BECAUSE THEY CHANGE THINGS. THEY PUSH THE HUMAN RACE FORWARD. AND WHILE SOME MAY SEE THEM AS THE CRAZY ONES, WE SEE GENIUS. BECAUSE THE PEOPLE WHO ARE CRAZY ENOUGH TO THINK THEY CAN CHANGE THE WORLD ARE **THE ONES WHO DO.**

STEVE JOBS

The world is filled with people who strive so hard to be loved by the majority that they lose all reason to love themselves. Humans are told since infancy that they must act a certain way, must dress in certain clothes, must say and do certain things, simply because that is what everyone does. These voices become subconscious wardens who command the minds of adults, leading them to make decisions based on what they have been told by others instead of what they have learned themselves. Far too many lives are wasted by choosing the monotony of safety over the boldness of the uncharted.

It is easy to travel upon a road laid by others but its only reward is the dust its builders leave behind. Have courage to pursue your own path. The greatest among us are most different from the rest.

MAN COULD NOT LIVE
IF HE WERE ENTIRELY
IMPERVIOUS TO
SADNESS.

MANY SORROWS
CAN BE ENDURED
ONLY BY BEING
EMBRACED.

EMILE DURKHEIM

Joy cannot exist without sadness. To truly know the bliss of happiness, a person must experience the aching of sorrow. Happiness is found in facing hardships and emerging victorious at the end.

The lowest times of life are periods of transition. Think back on struggles in your past and the strength you mustered to overcome them. You have succeeded before — you can succeed again. Welcome the sadness of life as times to reflect on where you are and where you wish to be. When standing at the bottom of a canyon, you have nowhere to climb but up.

SCIENCE
& BELIEF

A MAN SHOULD LOOK FOR WHAT IS AND NOT FOR WHAT HE THINKS SHOULD BE.

ALBERT EINSTEIN

Every person must approach science and belief with an open mind and a willingness to be proven wrong. There are no absolutes. Even in science, new theories replace old ones — even in religion, ancient practices are updated to conform to current understanding. Clinging to what you are convinced is true will only blind you to the truth in front of your eyes.

When searching for answers, leave all assumptions behind. Abandon all pre-conceptions and allow yourself to be incorrect. Look to discover truth only, even if it may disprove things you believe are un-questionable. If you seek truth, the sur-roundings may change but the foundation will remain the same.

FROM MAN OR ANGEL

THE GREAT ARCHITECT

DID WISELY
TO CONCEAL,
AND NOT DIVULGE
HIS SECRETS TO BE
SCANNED BY
THEM WHO OUGHT
RATHER ADMIRE

JOHN MILTON

It is impossible to prove the existence of a god; it is also impossible to prove there is no god either. The galaxy is filled with mysteries that even the brightest minds cannot explain. Were humans placed on Earth by a supernatural being? Are lives merely happenstance — the coincidental joining of molecules? Is there a purpose for life or is existence simply a temporary illusion?

Search for answers but be prepared to find them lacking. Some secrets are too complex for the human mind to comprehend. Some mysteries cannot be solved. Simply try to understand as much as you are able. Though beliefs between two people may stand on opposite ends of the spectrum, the truth is always found in the middle.

IN SCIENTIFIC WORK, THOSE WHO REFUSE TO GO BEYOND FACT RARELY GET AS FAR AS FACT.

THOMAS H. HUXLEY

The greatest discoveries begin with the simplest questions. Seekers look beyond what they are told is true for the mysteries that hide in places others have overlooked. Curiosity shines a spotlight on ideas that may appear solid but reveal hidden cracks when placed under scrutiny.

Do not rely on any foundation that seems unsteady. To find truth, you must never cease in asking questions and in doubting what you are told. Ignore those who ridicule you for your searching — before the ancient astronomers found their proof, millions of humans believed the Earth to be flat.

EVERYTHING
IN THE UNIVERSE
HAS A PURPOSE.
INDEED, THE
INVISIBLE
INTELLIGENCE
THAT FLOWS THROUGH
EVERYTHING
IN A PURPOSEFUL FASHION
IS ALSO FLOWING
THROUGH YOU

WAYNE DYER

There is a purpose for your life. It may be difficult to understand why you are here but the laws of the universe require a reason behind every existence. Every person, from the least to the greatest, is a unique mind with its own individual part to play in this universe's design. Though there are many colors in the grand tapestry of life, all people are equal strings.

You may feel as if you are lost in your own skin — unsure of where you are supposed to go and what you are supposed to do. But even the wisest spend their lives searching for this meaning. Even the wisest cannot fully answer this great conundrum.

Life is not about a beginning or an end. It is a journey of many steps. Only when you reach the end and look back will you finally see the full truth of your purpose.

'TIS THE OLD SECRET OF THE GODS THAT THEY COME IN LOW DISGUISES.

RALPH WALDO EMERSON

Humans cannot venture to understand the inner workings of the supernatural. Though the mind may be strong, the body that houses it is bound by the physical constraints of a physical brain. It is impossible for a creature that is natural to fully comprehend something that is not.

To be convinced, a human requires proof. Faith is a belief without proof. It relies on a person's ability to recognize their own physical limitations and to understand that some things simply cannot be explained. Even if they cannot prove something is real, they can believe in its possibility.

HEALTH &
HEALING

TAKE CARE OF
YOUR BODY WITH
STEADFAST FIDELITY.
THE SOUL MUST SEE
THROUGH THESE EYES
ALONE, AND IF THEY
ARE DIM, THE WHOLE
WORLD IS CLOUDED.

JOHANN WOLFGANG VON GOETHE

The body is the physical home of the mind. It is the machine that carries out your commands and the computer that processes data to make decisions. Wealth, power, happiness, and prestige can all be lost and survived, but the loss of a body is the loss of an existence.

There are no substitutes for the body you are born with. It can be improved and repaired but never replaced. Every choice you make is passed through it, and thus the quality of your decisions are directly affected by your body's condition. If you take care of your body, it will take care of you.

*IT TAKES MORE
THAN JUST A BODY
THAT LOOKS GOOD.
YOU MUST HAVE THE
HEART AND SOUL
TO GO WITH IT.*

EPICTETUS

A body is made stronger with exertion and effort. A mind is made stronger with learning and wisdom. A heart is made stronger with empathy and generosity. A soul is made stronger with a purpose and integrity. These are the core pieces of a human — the four elements that make life.

One is no more important than another. If you improve your body but not your mind, you will have strength but not the intelligence to use it. If you improve your heart but not your mind, you will be loved but cheated by deceivers. If you improve your mind but not your soul, you will gain all the rewards of wealth and power but find them to be meaningless. Care for you body, your mind, your heart, and your soul, and they will return your efforts in excess.

MANY PEOPLE
LOSE THEIR

HEALTH

SEEKING WEALTH,
AND THEN LOSE THEIR

WEALTH

SEEKING HEALTH.

ANONYMOUS

A wise entrepreneur balances short term and long term investments. Short term investments require effort now to return with a reward soon after — such as a job that is completed then paid for. Long term investments don't show results quickly, but add up over time and continue to produce rewards in perpetuity.

Your body is a long term investment. You must care for it a little each day so that it will produce returns forever. Of what purpose is it to gain all the wealth in the world only to stare at it from the confines of a hospital bed? Money cannot buy back the years spent in its pursuit. How many lifetimes are spent hoarding a fortune that cannot be buried with their bones?

IF A MAN ACHIEVES
VICTORY OVER HIS
BODY, WHO IN THE
WORLD CAN EXERCISE
POWER OVER HIM?
HE WHO RULES
HIMSELF RULES
OVER THE WHOLE
WORLD.

VINOBA BHAVE

The body is selfish. Its desire for pleasure and ease is so powerful that it can cloud the mind and affect decisions, leading even the strongest astray. How many kings have fallen because their bodies desired what was not theirs to take? How many emperors have lost their kingdoms in the reckless pursuit of what they wanted instead of what they needed? The body is a masterful manipulator and no poison is stronger than its whispers.

Learn to deny yourself. Step away from what you desire to see if it is truly what you need or merely an infatuation. A queen may defeat a thousand warriors and escape the wiles of a hundred assassins, but she is only as strong as the weakest part of her body.

REST

WHEN YOU ARE WEARY.

REFRESH

AND RENEW
YOURSELF,
YOUR BODY,
YOUR MIND,
YOUR SPIRIT.

THEN GET BACK TO WORK.

RALPH MARSTON

A person can spend a lifetime saving for the day when they can finally be happy, only to lose it all when their lifetime reaches its end. The journey of life is long and no one can see its final moment until it arrives. The pursuit of greatness is a gamble — one wrong move and all could be gone in an instant.

Work hard, but rest when you are able. Success is of no value if it is not enjoyed. Take time to enjoy the rewards of your victories and you will be encouraged to attain more.

LIFE &
DEATH

IN THE END, IT'S
NOT THE YEARS
IN YOUR LIFE
THAT COUNT.
IT'S THE LIFE
IN YOUR YEARS.

ABRAHAM LINCOLN

How do you want to be remembered after you die? Is your life filled with goals and dreams but not the actions required to reach them? Or is it a tale of achievements and glory but not the time required to enjoy them? You only have one life, so be wise in how you choose to live it.

Every person is a unique story. When faced with decisions, ask yourself which direction will make you happiest in ten years when the full picture has come into focus. Live as if today is the final chapter in your biography.

LIFE CAN ONLY BE

UNDERSTOOD

BACKWARDS,

BUT IT MUST

BE LIVED

FORWARD.

SOREN KIERKEGAARD

All decisions can be made better in hindsight. But time only ticks forward and mistakes in the past cannot be undone. Of what benefit is it to agonize over the missteps in your life? You cannot change the past. You cannot see the future. You can only change what is happening in the now.

You will make mistakes that you think can never be undone. It may seem easier to give up instead of trudging on through the storms of life, but it is only because your eyes cannot see beyond the murky horizon. When stranded in a desert, you cannot fall to your knees — you must stand and walk, and keep going until your very last breath. Though you cannot see over the hill ahead, it hides an ocean beyond its peak.

IT IS A WISE
MAN WHO
LIVES WITH

MONEY IN
THE BANK,

IT IS A FOOL
WHO DIES
THAT WAY.

ANONYMOUS

The value of money does not end at a life's conclusion. Generosity gives a person eternal life in the memories of those they provided comfort. Is it better to die with a net worth of billions but few remaining friends, or to change the lives of thousands who will miss you when you're gone?

Death is the great reset. The richest and the poorest both pass through its door — carrying nothing ahead, leaving everything behind. Wealth means nothing to the bones that used to own it. At life's end, only memories remain.

When you have much, give generously to those who do not. A million means little to those with billions; a penny means a lot to those who have none.

IN THE BOOK OF LIFE

EVERY PAGE HAS TWO

SIDES: WE HUMAN BEINGS

FILL THE UPPER SIDE WITH

OUR PLANS, HOPES

AND WISHES, BUT

PROVIDENCE WRITES

ON THE OTHER SIDE,

AND WHAT IT ORDAINS

IS SELDOM OUR GOAL.

NISAMI

You cannot control all things in life. You will strive for goals and never attain them. You will care for your body and it will fail you. You will love only to be hurt. Discouragement will poison your mind and divert you from the path. If you have done all in your power and still faltered, how can you ever hope for success?

Life is full of ups and downs. Take the hardships that life throws at you and use their tribulations to strengthen your armor. You cannot control the forces of chance, but it is always you who decides which direction to go.

LIFE IS A GREAT SURPRISE. *I DON'T SEE WHY DEATH SHOULD NOT BE AN EVEN* GREATER ONE

VLADIMIR NABOKOV

All creatures die. It is a fact that cannot be circumvented even by the wealthiest and most powerful. The end is always near — the clock is always counting down. Nothing you do will stop it.

Every story has a beginning, a middle, and an end. You cannot change the beginning and you cannot escape the end. You can only affect what happens in middle. Why worry about the end of your story when there are so many pages of life left to fill?

Death is not the end but merely the final door that a life passes through. What is beyond it? What journeys await you? As the final chapter closes, the book of life always begins again. Fear not for what is ahead.

ILLUMINATIONS

**WISDOM FROM THIS
PLANET'S GREATEST MINDS
ON TOPICS INCLUDING:**

POWER & LEADERSHIP

FAME & PRESTIGE

LOVE & RELATIONSHIPS

WEALTH & SUCCESS

KNOWLEDGE & WISDOM

CHOICES & DECISIONS

HARDSHIPS & BRAVERY

SCIENCE & BELIEF

HEALTH & HEALING

LIFE & DEATH

AND MORE

SECRETILLUMINATIONS.COM

THE
TALISMAN

THE **PYRAMID**

THE **LIGHT**

THE **EYE**

THE **ETERNAL CIRCLE**

LEARN MORE ABOUT THIS SYMBOL AT
ILLUMINATIONS1.COM/TALISMAN

52582380R00080

Made in the USA
Middletown, DE
19 November 2017